People
of the Past

PIONEER EDITION

By Kathy Burkett and Desmond Stills

CONTENTS

Ancient High-Rise.
Balcony House is one of hundreds of dwellings built into the cliffs of Mesa Verde National Park. At the edge of the site is a 600-foot drop.

About 700 years ago, a group of Native Americans lived in high cliffs. Then they disappeared.

PACIFIC
OCEAN

Utah   Colorado

Arizona

New Mexico

ATLANTIC
OCEAN

Gulf of Mexico

NATIONAL GEOGRAPHIC MAPS

ED

Four Corners.
Cliff dwellings exist throughout the Four Corners. That is the region where Utah, Colorado, New Mexico, and Arizona meet.

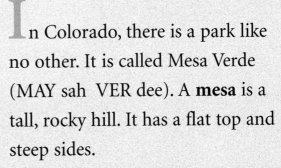

By Kathy Burkett

Life on the EDGE

In Colorado, there is a park like no other. It is called Mesa Verde (MAY sah VER dee). A **mesa** is a tall, rocky hill. It has a flat top and steep sides.

The park is best known for its ancient homes. They are carved into the **cliffs,** or steep sides, of the mesa. People made these homes hundreds of years ago.

Mesa Verde is not the only place with cliff homes. They are found throughout the **Four Corners.** That is the area where Colorado, New Mexico, Utah, and Arizona meet.

WHO LIVED IN THE CLIFFS?

No one knows for sure who lived here. But the Pueblo Indians have an idea. They think the people were their **ancestors.** Those are family members who lived long ago.

Scientists think the Pueblo may be right. The ancient homes look a lot like today's Pueblo homes. They are made with some of the same materials. They are even built in a similar way.

NATALIEJEAN/SHUTTERSTOCK.COM

Left: *The ancient people grew corn, beans, and squash on top of the mesas. They lived on the mesas until A.D. 1190.*
Center: *Then they moved into the cliffs.*
Right: *Around A.D. 1300 the people fled toward Mexico, New Mexico, and Arizona. There they built new homes and lives.*

MOVING TO THE CLIFFS

People began living in Mesa Verde around A.D. 570. At first, they lived on the tops of the mesas. But later they moved into the cliffs. No one knows why.

Maybe they wanted to farm on top of the mesas. So they moved off the land. Or maybe people feared an attack. Cliff homes might have been safer places to live.

LIFE IN MESA VERDE

Life in the cliffs was not easy. People had to climb down steep walls. They carved holes for their fingers and feet. Falling was always a risk.

Most homes were built near a **kiva**. That is a round underground room. People talked and told stories inside. They also held religious events. Pueblo today use kivas for many of the same things.

KINUKO Y. CRAFT/NATIONAL GEOGRAPHIC STOCK

FINDING FOOD

The ancient people lived in cliffs. But they farmed on top of mesas. They raised **crops,** or plants, to eat. They grew corn, beans, and squash. How do we know? Scientists found these plants in their homes.

The people also ate animals. Scientists found signs of hunting. They found rabbit and deer bones. They found bows and arrows too.

LEAVING HOME

People stopped building homes at Mesa Verde around A.D. 1300. They moved away. Scientists think they headed south toward Mexico, New Mexico, and Arizona.

No one has lived in Mesa Verde for hundreds of years. But for Pueblo Indians, the homes are not empty. They say their ancestors speak to them from the cliffs.

Digging **Hist**

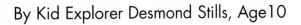

ory

By Kid Explorer Desmond Stills, Age 10

Have you ever wanted to travel back in time? I got that chance. A man named Joe McAvoy helped me. He is an archaeologist. He studies how people lived long ago.

I met McAvoy at Cactus Hill. That is a famous place in Virginia. About 30 years ago, a farmer found some spearpoints there.

Spearpoints are common in Cactus Hill. But these were different. They looked like points from Clovis, New Mexico.

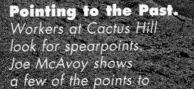

Pointing to the Past.
Workers at Cactus Hill look for spearpoints. Joe McAvoy shows a few of the points to Desmond Stills (right).

7

Digging in Time

The Clovis points are about 13,000 years old. People thought the earliest Americans made them. But the Cactus Hill points look older.

McAvoy studied them. It turns out they *are* older. They are the oldest ever found in the Americas.

People made the spearpoints about 18,000 years ago. Earth was in an ice age then. The world was a lot colder.

It was also dangerous. Many large animals lived near Cactus Hill. People had to watch out for wolves and bears. They hunted deer, elk, and mammoths.

A Big Change

The ice age people seemed to be doing fine. Then something happened. The climate changed. Earth got warmer. And the people of Cactus Hill disappeared. No one knows what happened to them.

McAvoy wants to find out. Maybe one day he will discover the answer. Maybe I can help!

MARGARET SIDLOSKY/NATIONAL GEOGRAPHIC STOCK

Making a Point. *Desmond Stills uses a deer antler to make a spearpoint.*

The Oldest Spearpoints

Cactus Hill
This stone spearpoint from Virginia is roughly 18,000 years old.

Clovis
These Clovis points were made about 13,000 years ago.

Chile
This spearpoint from Chile is as old as the Clovis points.

N O R T H

A M E R I C A

vis

Cactus Hill

How Did People Get to America?

They walked. That is what many scientists think. During the last ice age, Asia and North America were connected.

People probably first left Asia about 30,000 years ago. Over time, they spread across North and South America.

This map shows paths that the earliest Americans might have taken.

S O U T H

A M E R I C A

Map Key

Possible Paths

➤ 14,000 years ago

➤ 20,000 to 15,000 years ago

▪▪▪▪➤ 24,000 to 18,000 years ago

Vegetation and glaciation 21,000 years ago

- Forest
- Grassland, savanna, scrubland, tundra
- Desert
- Glacier

Some scientists wonder if people reached America in many different ways. How else might the first Americans have arrived?

9

Recorded in the Rings

When scientists study people of the past, they sometimes look at trees. Check out the stories tree rings can tell.

JIM BARBER/SHUTTERSTOCK.COM

Age Records

Each year, most trees grow a new layer of wood. It is just under the bark. These layers are called rings.

Each ring includes a light band and a dark band. The light band grows in the spring. The dark band grows in the summer and fall.

Weather Records

Trees grow wide rings in wet years. They grow narrow rings in dry years. Scientists study the patterns of tree rings (below). The patterns tell what the weather was like long ago. That is not all they can tell us.

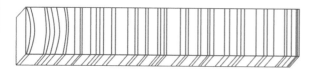

Dating Records

Scientists have studied living trees at Mesa Verde. One tree began growing in 1150 A.D. Scientists compared its rings with wood used in the cliff homes. They looked for matching patterns. A match tells them when a piece of wood was cut down. The cliff home was probably built soon afterward.

Tree Ring R⊙llup

Follow the directions below to make a model of a tree's rings.

Materials
- *ball of light–colored play dough*
- *ball of dark–colored play dough*
- *two sheets of waxed paper*
- *ruler*
- *rolling pin*
- *plastic knife*

Predict
- What will your model have in common with the rings on a real tree stump?
- How do you think it will it be different?

Test

1. Roll each ball of dough into a 10–inch rope. The dark rope should be as wide as a nickel. The light should be as wide as a quarter.

2. Place the dark rope on the waxed paper. Cover with a second piece of waxed paper.

3. Using a rolling pin, flatten the rope into a strip about 1 ¼ inches wide.

4. Set the dark strip aside. Repeat steps 2 and 3 with the light rope. This strip should be thicker than the first.

5. Cut ½ inch off the dark strip. Form that dough into a small tube. This shows your tree's first year of growth.

6. Place that tube at the end of your light strip. Roll until you have one layer of light dough around your tube (A). Cut the light dough. This layer shows early growth in your tree's second year.

7. Add a layer of dark play dough. It shows late growth during the tree's second year. Together, these two layers of growth make one tree ring (B).

8. Repeat Steps 6 and 7 to add two more years of growth to your model tree trunk.

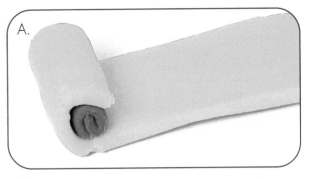

A.

B.

Conclude

9. Which way should you cut your model to show the rings inside?

10. Cut the model with a plastic knife.

11. How is your model like a real tree stump?

12. How is it different?

13. How old is your "tree"? (Hint: Don't forget to count the first year's growth.)

People of the Past

It is time to sample some questions and see what you have learned.

 What is Mesa Verde?

 What do cliff homes tell about the people who lived in them?

 What is special about the spearpoints at Cactus Hill?

 Why was the area of Cactus Hill dangerous 18,000 years ago?

 What can tree rings tell about the past?